TABLE OF CONTENTS

PROLOGUE
killer TIP #1 THE LESSONS OF HISTORY
killer TIP #2 MUSCLE MEMORY
killer TIP #3 MORE MUSCLE MEMORY
killer TIP #4 TABLE TENNIS IQ
killer TIP #5 MINDSET
killer TIP #6 GROWTH MINDSET, NOT FIXED MINDSET
killer TIP #7 MENTALITY
killer TIP #8 PREGAME RITUAL: CONFIDENCE
killer TIP #9 PREGAME RITUAL: FOCUS
killer TIP #10 LESS FEEDBACK IS MORE!
killer TIP #11 "QUIET EYE"
killer TIP #12 SERVING POWER
killer TIP #13 SERVING FACTS
killer TIP #14 SERVING TRICKS PART A
killer TIP #15 SERVING TRICKS PART B
killer TIP #16 SERVING TRICKS PART C
killer TIP #17 RECEIVING TRICKS

"It's not the strongest nor the fastest athlete who survives. But the one who is most responsive to change."

KILLERTIPS NETWORK
http://killertips.net

killer TIP #18 GAME PLAN A & GAME PLAN B
killer TIP #19 DISTRACTION & DECEPTION: BALL NOT IN PLAY
killer TIP #20 DISTRACTION & DECEPTION: BALL IN PLAY
killer TIP #21 THE PHYSICS OF PADDLE: SWEET SPOTS
killer TIP #22 THE PHYSICS OF PADDLE: QUADRANT
killer TIP #23 MYTH BUSTER
killer TIP #24 TRAJECTORY & APOGEE
killer TIP #25 THE ANATOMY OF TOPSPIN & BACKSPIN
killer TIP #26 SIDESPIN SIDE EFFECTS
killer TIP #27 "DANCING WITH THE STARS"
killer TIP #28 THE CHAMPION'S MIND PART A
killer TIP #29 THE CHAMPION'S MIND PART B
killer TIP #30 THE CHAMPION'S MIND PART C
killer TIP #31 SERVING PRACTICE
killer TIP #32 RECEIVING PRACTICE
EPILOGUE

Copyright © 2019 by *Killertips* Network.

All rights reserved. No part of this publication may be used or reproduced, stored in a retrieval system or transmitted in any form or by any means, electronic, mechanical, photocopying, recording, scanning, or otherwise, except as permitted under Section 107 or 108 of the 1976 United States Copyright Act, without written permission.

Killertips Network
Editor in Chief: Lizbeth Sharon

ISBN: 978-0-578-49797-6

Library of Congress Control Number: 2019940070

Printed in the USA, UK, and Australia

PROLOGUE

COACH CAI ZHENHUA:

It is a fact that having won as many as 140 gold, 102 silver, and 153 bronze medals as of 2018, no other team in the table tennis world is as highly decorated as the Chinese National Team (CNT).

Not even close!

The CNT is the de facto "Boston Celtics" of table tennis in the past and the "Golden State Warriors" of table tennis in the present.

They are absolutely the team to beat!

Coach Cai Zhenhua once ordered his army: "Win at all costs!"

TABLE TENNIS killer TIPS

"WIN AT ALL COSTS!"

Until the rest of the world go back to the drawing board and constantly:

#1. RETHINK each and every fundamental of table tennis

#2. REDESIGN each and every player's mindset .....

..... until they are fully COMMITTED to whatever it takes to win .....

..... until they ultimately bring that CHANGE to the table .....

the CNT will continue to dominate the people's republic of table tennis for a very long time.

killer TIPS NETWORK

> "Those who do not learn history are doomed to repeat it."

killer TIP #1
THE LESSONS OF HISTORY

killer TIP #1

It is a fact that table tennis is China's national sport as declared by Chairman Mao Zedong, the communist leader and the founder of the People's Republic of China, in the early 1950s.

The leader wanted his people to be motivated, confident, and successful in the sport, and it has since become an integral part of China's identity and patriotism.

Table tennis or ping-pong, has proven to be politically correct for the leader and socially correct for his 1.4 billion people.

Table tennis is a budget, space, and physically-friendly sport.

TABLE TENNIS killer TIPS

THE LESSONS OF HISTORY

There are tables in nearly every park and nearly every school has a team that trains on regular basis.

People of all ages are able to play, from 9-year young babies to 90-year old grannies.

Rumor has it that 10 million Chinese play in tournaments regularly and some 300 million play occasionally.

According to Matthew Syed, a former Commonwealth champion, the sport has proven to help a lot with China's domestic politics.

The Chinese government claimed everything was fantastic because China is winning in table tennis!

killer **TIPS NETWORK**

"I fear not the man who has practiced 10,000 kicks one time. I fear the man who has practiced one kick 10,000 times."

killer TIP #2
MUSCLE MEMORY

killer TIP #2

Zhang Zhihe began playing the sport at the age of two under the coaching of his parents, who were both former professional players.

When he was 13, his parents sent him to a sports academy.

At the age of 14 years and 61 days in 2017, he became the youngest ever winner of an ITTF World Tour Men's Singles title!

As of January 2019, this 15-year-old boy ranked at #3 in the world.

The table tennis community across the globe recognizes him as Tomokazu Harimoto, a naturalized citizen of Japan.

TABLE TENNIS killer TIPS

MUSCLE MEMORY

Steph Curry of the Golden State Warriors shot his first basketball at five and had never stopped shooting ever since. Today he is arguably the sharpest-shooter in NBA history.

The Chinese netizens nickname him "F*cks the Sky".

Facts have proven that the longer and more often your muscles perform certain tasks, the quicker, the smoother, the more precise, and the more automatic the results will be.

These finely coordinated muscle movements are called "muscle memory".

However, rather than in the muscles, the process of memorizing actually happens in the brain.

killer **TIPS NETWORK**

"Practice makes permanent."

killer TIP #3

MORE MUSCLE MEMORY

killer TIP #3

Compared to other racket sports like tennis and badminton, table tennis doesn't have a record-breaking ball speed.

However, due to its smaller size, light weight, bounce rate, and spin potential, the average speed of a table tennis ball could be higher than the ball speeds of those other two.

Not to mention the much smaller table-sized court!

The interval between one hit and the next is shorter.

This gives you a lower response time on average due to the characteristics of the ball and the court size.

TABLE TENNIS killer TIPS

MORE MUSCLE MEMORY

Imagine a bouncy, fast, and spinny ball moving back and forth above such a small surface and caught between two fast hands of two opposing players.

Those are the fundamentals that makes table tennis a game of exceptional coordination and reflex.

A game that relies mainly on sophisticated motor skills. A game that is exceptionally repetitive. A game that has a metronome-like tempo. A game that is so "robotic"!

Watch the clip at: bit.ly/2FZTUMh

"Muscle memory"—that's where the CNT invests their money in the sport!

killer TIPS NETWORK

"The measure of intelligence is the ability to change."

killer TIP #4
TABLE TENNIS IQ

killer TIP #4

There's Soccer IQ, Basketball IQ, Football IQ, Baseball IQ, etc.

IQ (Intelligence Quotient) indicates how well and how quickly someone uses information and logic to answer questions and make predictions.

IQ represents abilities such as visual or eye skills, spatial skills, problem solving skills, retention and memory, multitasking, etc.

Kobe Bryant, who reportedly has the highest intelligence and was the most tenacious player in the NBA, once defined Basketball IQ as "the ability to read one another and read the defense very quickly".

TABLE TENNIS killer TIPS

TABLE TENNIS IQ

Now, what is table tennis IQ?

It's the ability to recognize an opponent's moves, logically respond to them, then consequently make predictions and adjustments necessary towards that opponent's next moves at game speed.

Players with high table tennis IQ know how to utilize their EYES timely, accurately, and continuously. So, IQ could be written as "EyeQ"!

Inaccurate visualization, such as misreading spins or moves on an opponent's serves, pushes, flicks, chops, etc. will only mislead the brain into miscoordinating muscle movements and so forth.

killer **TIPS NETWORK**

"Your table tennis greatness is only as good as your mindset."

killer TIP #5
MINDSET

killer TIP #5

Dr. Stan Beecham, a sports psychologist who has been working with the best of the best from all over the world in the last 25 years, has said:

"The primary determinant of success is MINDSET.
NOT talent. NOT experience."

What is mindset?
It is a set of BELIEFS about yourself and what you can achieve.

If you believe that you can jump high enough to touch the lamp on the ceiling, you'll likely try your best to prove it.

If you believe that you can't, you won't even try!

TABLE TENNIS killer TIPS

MINDSET

At the beginning of every new NBA season, if you asked any player—either from the best to the worst team in the league—about his goal, you'll hear similar answer:

"TO BECOME THE CHAMPIONS!"

Until you believe that you can win, you'll surely lose. Until you have that positive mindset, your achievement in the sport won't go anywhere.

Your mind is the "general" and your body is its "army". The latter follows as far as the former goes.

Because your mind in fact controls your body, your performance in sports relies 100% on the mind.

killer **TIPS NETWORK**

"Find a way or make one!"

# *killer* TIP #6

GROWTH MINDSET, NOT FIXED MINDSET

killer TIP #6

World-renowned Stanford University psychologist and one of the world's leading researchers in the field of motivation, Carol Dweck, Ph.D, has presented two types of mindsets:

#1. FIXED MINDSET:
You believe your intelligence, talents, skills, etc. are fixed.
So, you resist learning and resist improving them.

#2. GROWTH MINDSET:
You believe you can still improve and develop whatever you have through learning, hard work, and persistence.

Your mindset can motivate you to fulfill your potential or prevent you from doing so!

TABLE TENNIS killer TIPS

GROWTH MINDSET, NOT FIXED MINDSET

It's possible that athletes with fixed mindsets could be superstars in college basketball, in table tennis provincial teams, or even in the CNT!

However, they don't believe they can step up to the next level, learn anything new, learn from mistakes, make adjustments, develop, and keep improving.

Because of this, a lot of NBA teams who drafted superstars from the NCAA end up with "busts" because those players were practically done after college!

They believed the college level was their plateau. So, they never brought their "A" game to the pros because their best had been left in college.

killer TIPS NETWORK

"Fall seven times, stand up eight."

killer TIP #7
MENTALITY

Killer TIP #7

The way professional athletes perform is very important.

The way professional coaches perform is very important, too.

However, their performance is not more important than what their beliefs are!

This is because the way they play and the way they coach are reflective of what they believe.

Regardless of whether they have ever signed a "declaration of war" against the CNT, what they truly believe is what they will ultimately live out.

TABLE TENNIS *killer* TIPS

MENTALITY

What is mentality?

It is a way of thinking and an attitude derived from a mindset.
So, positive mindset generates positive mentality and vice versa.

If Miu Hirano has a Growth Mindset, she believes she'll keep learning, improving, and fighting.
That's a winning mentality!

Kobe Bryant on his so-called "Mamba Mentality":

"Mamba Mentality means the ability to constantly try to be the best version of yourself. It's a constant quest to try to be better today than you were yesterday."

killer **TIPS NETWORK**

"Confidence is silent, insecurities are loud."

killer TIP #8

PREGAME RITUAL: CONFIDENCE

Killer TIP #8

In table tennis, where the ball is one of the bounciest, fastest, and spinniest moving objects on the smallest court in sports, you simply can't afford any form of distraction.

You can lose a point in a split second and lose a match in a few minutes.

As a professional, you practice a lot more than you compete in tournaments.

Your body already knows what to do because your table tennis skillset is already there.

Your skillset certainly won't get any better in tournaments.

TABLE TENNIS killer TIPS

PREGAME RITUAL: CONFIDENCE

However, it can get worse if you're less confident and less focused!

In tournaments, you should never worry about your your strokes and your footwork. That belongs in training, not in tournaments.

You don't "THINK". You BELIEVE!

You think, you'll sink.
You blink, you'll stink.

On the court, champions don't even try to think. They're just confident that they'll do well.

Consequently, they never try to give their opponents any confidence. They try to take it at all times!

killer TIPS NETWORK

"Look at a stone cutter hammering away at his rock, perhaps 100 times without as much as a crack showing in it. Yet at the 101 blow, it will split in two, and I know it was not the last blow that did it, but all that had gone before."

killer TIP #9

PREGAME RITUAL: FOCUS

killer TIP #9

Always take advantage of warmups to get physically and mentally focused.

Physically, warming up prepares your heart, lungs, and muscles:

#1. As your muscles get warmer, your body temperature also increases. This will improve muscle elasticity, which enhances power and speed while reducing the risk of injury due to overstretching.

#2. Warming up also helps your shoulders and knees reach the maximum movement capacity.

Now, mental focus starts with nothing but your EYES:

TABLE TENNIS killer TIPS

PREGAME RITUAL: FOCUS

#1. When the ball is not rolling, take time to gaze at the whole table surface at all times.

Like a digital camera, your eyes will take a "snapshot" of it then save this "image" in your mind. So, it'll always remind your motor system where to play.

#2. When the ball is in play, gaze at and follow the ball at all times.

Your brain is like a GPS. When your eyes input data, it will map the target, distance, path, tempo, etc.

So, turn your eyes on the ball at all times and everything else will strangely become a blur!

killer **TIPS NETWORK**

"Until your one thing is done, everything else is a distraction."

killer TIP #10
LESS FEEDBACK IS MORE!

Killer TIP #10

Hey coaches, don't you know that the less you tell your players in a tournament, the better your players perform in there?

Evidence-based research and empirical findings prove that less feedback is actually better for competition. That's the general consensus over an overwhelming majority of research findings.

As a matter of fact, feedback could become counterproductive since it's potentially distracting or defocusing.

The match between Guo Yue of China and Li Jiawei of Singapore in 2008 is a GOOD example of a BAD practice of dealing with feedback.

TABLE TENNIS Killer TIPS

LESS FEEDBACK IS MORE!

In the sixth game where Li Jiawei was trailing 2-3 in the match, TV spectators could clearly see some Chinese handwriting on her left palm that read like "PATIENCE".

Watch the clip at: bit.ly/2OQq8wa

So, whenever Li served, that reminder or "feedback" was always made visible to her.

However, playing a game full of distraction, deception, fast and spinny balls on a tiny court, fast arms, fast hands, fast wrists—not to mention against the CNT—, it has been proven that any ADDITION of feedback could result in the SUCTRACTION of any athlete's focus.

---

killer TIPS NETWORK

> "You are
> quiet,
> but you are
> not blind."

killer TIP #11
"QUIET EYE"

killer TIP #11

In the NBA, some players successfully shoot only 39% of their free throws, while others make 93% of theirs.

What makes one player such a sharpshooter while another has more trouble making a basket?

A new finding has indicated that it's actually the visual and cognitive skills which determine coordination, more so than just physical prowess.

This means your EYE SKILLS trump your physicality!

This is known as the "quiet-eye" theory, which originated from Professor John Vickers in the 1980s.

TABLE TENNIS killer TIPS

"QUIET EYE"

Here's the application of the "quiet-eye" technique in table tennis strokes, especially serves:

Before you serve, focus your gaze on the salient aspects of your goal, such as the thin white line on the middle (useful in doubles); or any white line on the left edge, on the back edge, on the right edge, on the left corner, or on the right corner of your opponent's court.

This "eye habit" will dramatically help your motor system gain laser focus and pinpoint accuracy on the table!

This technique has been proven and tested for improved performance in basketball shooting, in golf, in marksmanship, and even in surgery.

killer **TIPS NETWORK**

"Plan your attack and attack your plan!"

killer TIP #12
SERVING POWER

Killer TIP #12

Since serves are granted the right to put the ball in play or to get the point started, serves inherently have a STRIKE-FIRST power as shown:

#1. The server, has 100% control of the ball while the receiver has 0% control of the ball because:

- The server KNOWS while the receiver SPECULATES

- Serve is an "execution-style" shot! The server EXECUTES and the receiver is being EXECUTED

#2. Due to having the HIGHEST percentage of control, serving has the LOWEST percentage of unforced errors.

TABLE TENNIS Killer TIPS

SERVING POWER

#3. The possession of the "100% control of the ball", or the serve, is GUARANTEED for each opposing side at least 6X per game.

#4. The server has TWO chances to score:

Chance #1: With ace, serve winners, or unforced errors on the receiver's part

Chance #2: With the follow-up shot or so-called "3rd ball attack" after the serve is successfully returned

#5. Table tennis has, quite literally, the "edge" in lucky edge balls ("money balls"), unlike other racket sports such as tennis or badminton.

"If you close your eyes to facts, you will learn through disasters."

killer TIP #13
SERVING FACTS

killer TIP #13

Jan Magnus and Franc Klaassen, who analyzed data on 481 matches:

"The probability of players that serve and end up winning the point is 64.4% in the men's singles and 56.1% in the women's singles."

Carl Bialik, who compiled Rio 2016 Olympic's data on 100's of matches:

"#1. In tennis, the probability of a server who ends up winning the point is 63% in the men's singles and 57% in the women's singles.

#2. In table tennis, the probability of a server who ends up winning the point is 53% in the men's singles and 53% in the women's singles."

TABLE TENNIS killer TIPS

SERVING FACTS

In table tennis, serving facts on court have proven to be in line with serving fundamentals on paper.

Theoretically, it is advantageous.

However, this advantage is not put to PRACTICE but rather to PARADOX.

"An advantage that is not taken advantage of."

Serves prove to be often used as a weapon in tennis, but not so much in table tennis. It's rarely taken advantage of to finish points off:

Aces —> bit.ly/2X0C1mn
Winners —> bit.ly/2I5Qgmx
Unforced errors —> bit.ly/2XpclzU

---

killer **TIPS NETWORK**

"Creativity is intelligence having fun, so serve creatively! The creative zone no athlete has ever been."

killer TIP #14
SERVING TRICKS
PART A

killer TIP #14

#1. Facts have proven that servers are more likely to get away with the first two points in a match because the receivers are more like in learning mode, not attacking mode.

#2. So, it is advisable to elect to serve rather than to receive when you win the toss in a match.

#3. If you're serving to open a brand new match, always serve the first one SHORT 'N LOW WITH TOPSPIN. It's because psychologically, at the very beginning of a match, players tend to be a little overcautious. So, in this case, receivers will be more than likely to overreact toward the incoming serve of the match.

TABLE TENNIS killer TIPS

SERVING TRICKS PART A

#4. Even for the second serve of the match, receivers are still likely to be a bit sluggish. So, a faster serve but deep on the other side of the receiver's end will have a potential ace!

#5. In serves, spin variation matters but tempo variation does too! Variation of slow and fast serves can seriously disrupt your opponent's rhythm.

#6. Serve differently each time. No players expect to be burnt twice. If their first return hits the net, it's unlikely that they make similar mistake due to a lesson learned. So, if the second serve is similar to the first one, it'll be more likely to be returned correctly than if it has different spin, speed, and placement.

killer TIPS NETWORK

"**Creativity is a work ethic. It takes courage!**"

killer TIP #15
SERVING TRICKS PART B

Killer TIP #15

#1. The friendliest serve spin for good 3rd ball attack is with minimum topspin or no spin. It's always harder to attack a returned ball containing backspin or maximum topspin.

#2. The safest serve placement is short 'n low on the middle line. Both right-handed and left-handed players find it harder to attack from either side of the table.

#3. The best serve spin and placement is topspin but short 'n low on the middle line. A serve that lands low but close to the net is tricky to return. If it's attacked, the "low" ball may hit the "high" net that's close to it. If it's blocked, the ball may fly off the table due to its topspin and angle.

TABLE TENNIS killer TIPS

SERVING TRICKS PART B

#3. The best serving position is on the middle line because:

* The opposing players tend to stand diagonally. If the server moves to the middle, the receiver will likely to some adjustment. In fact, straight court distance is shorter (9' vs 10.3'), causing lower margin of error for the receiver. Let alone the 0% control!

* While serving from left corner tends to land the ball somewhere diagonally on the receiver's court, serving from the middle of the table is more unpredictable.

* Serving from the middle of the table gives more equal comfort for either forehand or backhand serves.

killer TIPS NETWORK

"You can never use up creativity. The more you use, the more you have."

killer TIP #16
SERVING TRICKS PART C

killer TIP #16

#1. Add a new serving position such as the middle to vary your serves.

#2. Always make your upcoming serve a secret and make the receiver speculate. Unlike tennis and badminton, table tennis allows serves from ANYWHERE to ANYWHERE.

However, facts have proven that most players rarely take advantage of this.

Serving with forehand on the left side is becoming "generic" in table tennis today. It's getting MORE predictable and LESS speculation on the receivers!

In fact, before serving, always be on standby in the MIDDLE of the table. Once your opponent's ready, decide where you want to serve FROM!

TABLE TENNIS killer TIPS

SERVING TRICKS PART C

#3. Serving in table tennis is like High Jump in "Track and Field".
"Where you jump" determines "where you'll land". Where the ball bounces determines where it'll land.
So, it's your serve' FIRST BOUNCE that matters!

The closer the first bounce to the net, the closer the landing to the net and vice versa. So, the net is kind of a "mirror"!

#4. Take advantage of your serve to set the tempo of the point's rally. Although receivers can flick your serves etc, the serve speed tends to determine the rest of the rally's tempo.

FASTER SERVES tend to be followed by FASTER RALLIES and vice versa.

killer TIPS NETWORK

> "Losing is
> no big deal.
> Winning is
> the trick."

killer TIP #17
RECEIVING TRICKS

killer TIP #17

If the server has the MAXIMUM chance to score a point in the game, then the receiver has the MINIMUM chance to score a point.

The server's double chances are:

#1. A point off the serve
#2. A point off the 3rd ball attack

Advisedly, as the receiver:

#1. Gaze at the FOUR CORNERS of the court before the server tosses the ball

#2. Once it's tossed, focus your attention on the ball and see the CONTACT SPOT ON THE BALL, not the server's hand.
The lower the contact spot, the more backspin and vice versa.

TABLE TENNIS killer TIPS

RECEIVING TRICKS

#3. Always try to find ways to ATTACK serves. At least, try to return more aggressively or unpredictably in order to avoid 3rd ball attack from the server

* attack from behind your court

* if it's inaccessible, try from either side of your court for shorter and easier reach to the incoming serve.

#4. If attacking is not a good option:

* return it with sidespin due to its topspin and backspin mixture

bit.ly/2KCgfnw

- just deflect the ball without imparting any spin in order to PRESERVE the server's spin (*"Return to Sender"*)

killer TIPS NETWORK

"If the plan doesn't work, change the plan. But never the goal."

killer TIP #18
GAME PLAN A & GAME PLAN B

killer TIP #18

What is a Game Plan?
It is an action or series of actions on how to score in the game.

What is Game Plan A?
It is the preferred scoring method due to its efficiency, defined as achieving maximum productivity with minimum expense or wasted effort.

What is Game Plan B?
It is a scoring method that can be used if Game Plan A is neutralized.

The scoring effectiveness of these plans relies on each of your serves.

NEVER toss the ball up into the air until you have your Game Plan A and Game Plan B READY TO GO:

TABLE TENNIS *killer* TIPS

GAME PLAN A & GAME PLAN B

#1. If your're serving, execute your Game Plan A first to try to SCORE off the ace, winner, or unforced error. If it manages to score, keep it up.

#2. If it doesn't, kick Game Plan B in and try to finish the point. However, if it is still unable to close it out, continue the rally AGGRESSIVELY.

#3. If Game Plan A proves to be ineffective, either because it's difficult to score off the serve or with the 3rd ball attack, SKIP OVER it using Game Plan B all the way.

Benjamin Franklin:
"If you fail to plan, you plan to fail."

NO game plans, NO serves!

killer TIPS NETWORK

"Starve your distractions. Feed your focus."

killer TIP #19
DISTRACTION & DECEPTION: BALL NOT IN PLAY

Killer TIP #19

In one of the world's fastest, spinniest, and smallest-court sports, distraction and deception are crucially legal to the game.

Any glimpse of distraction—from foot-stomping when serving, to hand-wiggling after serving—could turn into deception on the opponent, from the spin to the trajectory of the ball, etc.

No other sport has such distracting serves like table tennis does!

Distraction is a means to create deception in an opponent's eyes. You deceive your opponents by legally distracting them at the table.

TABLE TENNIS killer TIPS

DISTRACTION & DECEPTION: BALL NOT IN PLAY

You can hardly cheat your opponents' minds. However, you can manipulate their visual!

Distracted eyes could lead into deceived eyes, resulting in deceived coordination on the opponent's end.

When the ball is not in play, always gaze at the entire table surface at all times to refresh and to update the PHOTOGRAPHIC MEMORY of your "battlefield".

"If the light will go off in five seconds, you should 'check' your surroundings, such as the position of objects near you, the door, the way there, etc."

This is all useful DATA for your motor system!

killer TIPS NETWORK

"The greatest deception athletes suffer is from their own perceptions."

killer TIP #20
DISTRACTION & DECEPTION: BALL IN PLAY

killer TIP #20

As soon as the ball is tossed up into the air, make sure to keep your eyes locked on the ball AT ALL TIMES.

That's how to fend off any kind of distraction and deception when the ball is in play.

Here is the 2017 ITTF Handbook on "The Laws of Table Tennis" (the most current version):

2.5.7 "A player strikes the ball if he or she touches it in play with:

#1. his or her racket, held in the hand,

#2. his or her racket hand below the wrist."

DISTRACTION & DECEPTION: BALL IN PLAY

So, until the ITTF revises this law, it is legal to hit the ball with ANYTHING BELOW the playing hand, from the rubber surface and any part of the racket to any part of the hand under the wrist.

Go practice striking the ball, especially on SHORT serves and pushes, also net plays with:

#1. the racket's handle
#2. the racket's edge
#3. any knuckle of your fingers

It's 100% guaranteed to be distractingly deceptive and disturbing, but not disapproved by the ITTF.

So, #1, #2, #3 are perfectly LEGAL!

killer TIPS NETWORK

> "*Error analysis is the sweet spot for improvement.*"

killer TIP #21
THE PHYSICS OF PADDLE: SWEET SPOTS

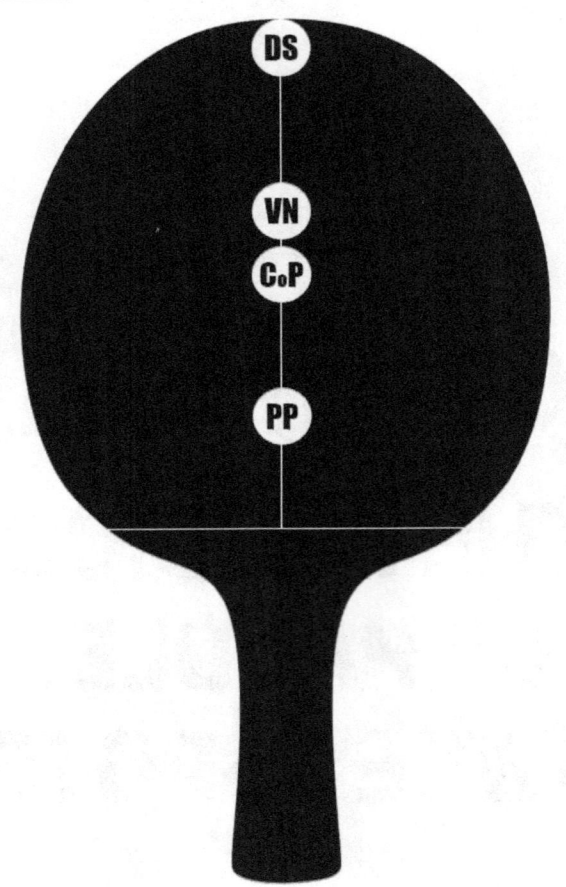

DS = Dead Spot
VN = Vibration Node
CoP = Center of Percussion
PP = Power Point

THE PHYSICS OF PADDLE: SWEET SPOTS

The Dead Spot is a point near the tip of the paddle that gives the ball minimum to ZERO BOUNCE.
It's the best spot to serve from, but the worst to receive serves.

The Vibration Node is a point with ZERO VIBRATION. This is one of the sweet spots due to its minimum loss of the paddle's energy to vibration.

The Center of Percussion is a sweet spot due to its BALANCED position that adds stability upon ball contact.

The Power Point is another sweet spot where the ball achieves the MOST BOUNCE upon contact.
Since it provides the best control of the ball, it is an ideal spot to receive serves.

killer **TIPS NETWORK**

"Athletes don't strike at every ball. They look for the balls in the strike zone."

killer TIP #22
THE PHYSICS OF PADDLE: QUADRANT

Killer TIP #22

Q2 = Right-handed power spot
Q3 = Right-handed control spot
Q1 = Left-handed power spot
Q4 = Left-handed control spot

TABLE TENNIS *Killer* **TIPS**

THE PHYSICS OF PADDLE: QUADRANT

For both right-handed and left-handed players, Quadrant 2 and Quadrant 1 provide more POWER due to being closer to the tip, which provides higher momentum transfer of energy.

For both right-handed and left-handed players, Quadrant 3 and Quadrant 4 provide more CONTROL due to being closer to the hand, which provides higher sensitivity.

Not only do Q2 & Q3 provide the best hitting areas for righties and Q1 & Q4 for lefties, these quadrants can also easily LIFT backspin and return LOW balls due to quadrant location on the BOTTOM or LOWER HALF, not the top or higher half of the paddle.

killer TIPS NETWORK

"Nothing is harder than competing with a myth."

killer TIP #23
MYTH BUSTER

killer TIP #23

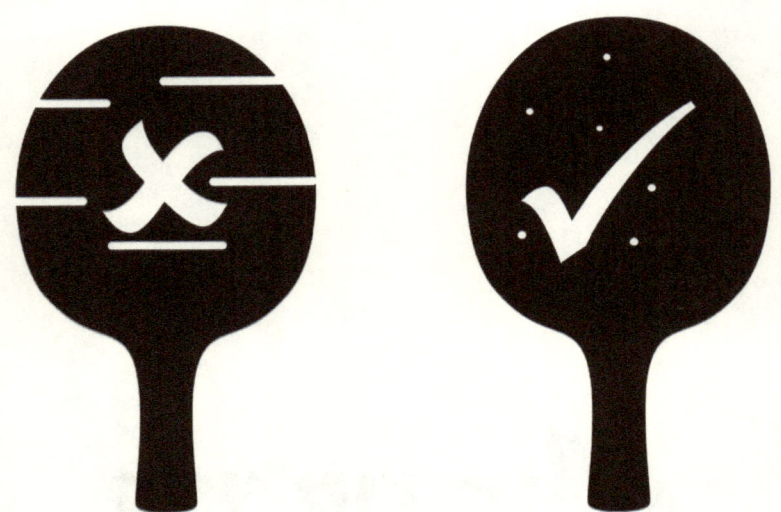

MYTH:
When imparting topspin or backspin on the ball with loops or serves, roll the ball on the rubber surface.

FACT:
There's no evidence that the ball rolls on the rubber surface when it's being spun. There are never "line markings" on the rubber surface and on the ball, but rather dot ones only!

TABLE TENNIS killer **TIPS**

MYTH BUSTER

The ball always bounces back mid-air as soon as it "grabs" the spin from the rubber surface.

There's no time for rolling nor skidding on the rubber, unless there's some "liquid" on it.

You must spin the ball on the right quadrant of your paddle, not roll it across the quadrant.

If the ball looks as if it's dragging across the rubber surface, it's just a follow-through motion of the stroke that's also found in serving.

In fact, this is what really happens:

bit.ly/2ZbbyUY

---

killer TIPS NETWORK

> "Fight your stagnation. Change your trajectory."

killer TIP #24
TRAJECTORY & APOGEE

Killer TIP #24

TRAJECTORY is the path travelled by the ball after being struck by a player, up until it lands across the court.

APOGEE is the highest vertical point on a trajectory.

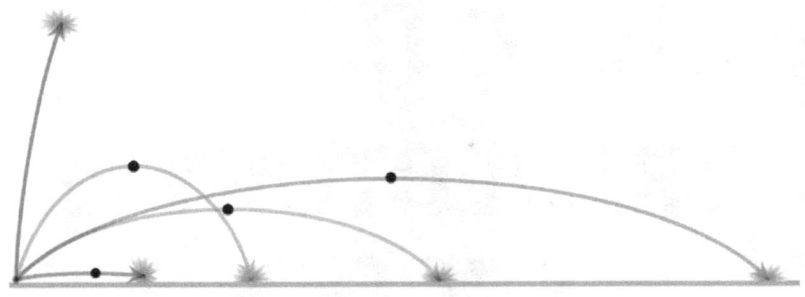

Rule #1. The SOONER the ball reaches its apogee, the SOONER the ball will land.

Rule #2. The LOWER the apogee of the ball, the LOWER the ball will bounce after landing

TABLE TENNIS killer TIPS

TRAJECTORY & APOGEE

Pay attention to HOW SOON and HOW LOW the apogee was reached for a perfect landing.

An example of PERFECT apogee by Lee Chong Wei of Malaysia:

bit.ly/2HZQs6G

Whenever you loop, flick, or push, make sure the ball's apogee is STILL above your own court.

If it has crosssed the net and is already above your opponent's court, the ball will more likely go off the table.

Or at least, it'll give your opponent more time to respond to your shot.

---

killer **TIPS NETWORK**

> "Cross the loud river, but don't cross the silent one."

killer TIP #25
THE ANATOMY OF TOPSPIN & BACKSPIN

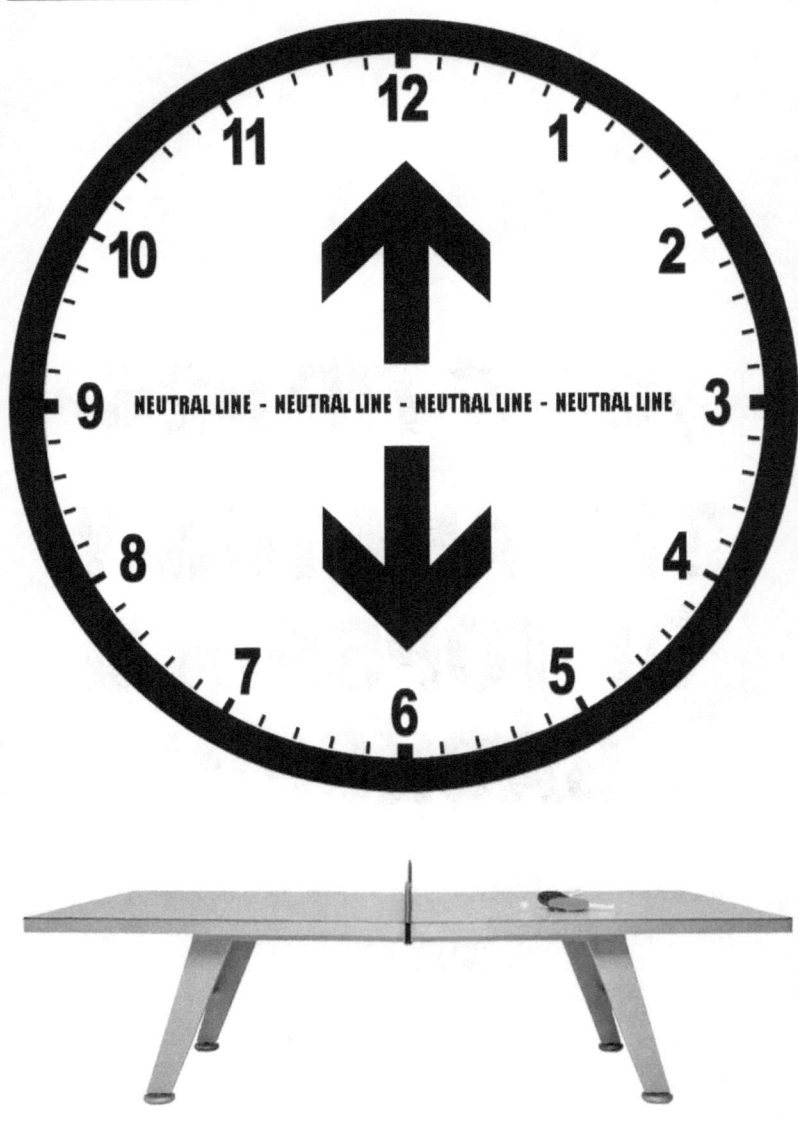

KILLER TIP #25

TABLE TENNIS KILLER TIPS

THE ANATOMY OF TOPSPIN & BACKSPIN

Assume you're on the right and your opponent is on the left of the table:

#1. The HIGHER the contact spot on the ball (3-12 o'clock), the SPINNIER the TOPSPIN.

#2. The LOWER the contact spot on the ball (3-6 o'clock), the SPINNIER the BACKSPIN.

#3. If your contact spot is between 6-9 o'clock, the ball will bounce "BACK" to you.

#4. The 3 o'clock spot has the highest momentum AGAINST you. So, try to avoid a FRONTAL contact on the ball and instead go for the SIDE. Getting "sideswiped" isn't as bad as getting hit by a "car's bumper", is it?

killer TIPS NETWORK

"Don't look where you fell, but where you slipped."

killer TIP #26

SIDESPIN SIDE EFFECTS

killer TIP #26

It is a fact that table tennis is dominated by topspin rallies with quick forearms, fast hands, and snappy wrists; ON and CLOSE to the table.

Spin variation, however, has proven to be strangely uninspiring in the sport as per Rio 2016 Olympics' data.

In fact, less spinny sports like baseball and soccer prove to have taken more advantage of the spin.

While table tennis only recognizes topspin, backspin, and sidespin balls, baseball has more variation— fastballs, curveballs, sliders, slurves, knuckle balls, and more.

bit.ly/2KoooM5
bit.ly/2HUy1Ak

TABLE TENNIS killer TIPS

SIDESPIN SIDE EFFECTS

Sidespin is, in fact, the most majestic spin of all. Its mixture of topspin and backspin makes it more unpredictable.

It swirls and disrupts the tempo.

Sidespin can break or alter a rally and stretch the court!

Wider angle will FORCE the opponent to reach for the ball, move away from the table, then hit SIDEWAYS.

Unlike tennis athletes, table tennis players are NOT engineered to "sprint" and "run around" the court as much:

bit.ly/2Z5kTgZ

ALWAYS hit the ball AWAY FROM your opponent's forearm, hand, and wrist!

killer TIPS NETWORK

"Stop looking for points in the same place you lost them."

killer TIP #27
"DANCING WITH THE STARS"

killer TIP #27

Dancers and athletes have something in common:

If there's slow-tempo dance, there's fast-tempo dance.
If there's slow-tempo game, there's fast-tempo game.

A great Salsa (150-250 beats per minute) dancer is not automatically a great Rumba (128-144 beats per minute) dancer and vice versa.

It's all because their performance operates under their certain tempo. The two work hand in hand.

Changing the tempo may change the performance, especially in a game as fast as and as spinny as table tennis.

TABLE TENNIS killer TIPS

"DANCING WITH THE STARS"

Timo Boll admires Ma Lin due to his table tennis IQ! Ma Lin's ability to adjust his game at the right timing, from tactic to tempo, is second to none!

When his opponents were in a scoring spree, he slowed down the game dramatically. As soon as his opponent started to adjust to "Rumba", Ma Lin stormed out with "Salsa" and vice versa. All in game speed!

Fast-tempo athletes may become impatient and defocused when they are forced to slow down and vice versa.

When fast-tempo opponents are about to serve, give a signal and ask to wait until you're "ready". Try to slow them down in order to CONTROL their pace.

killer **TIPS NETWORK**

"If my mind can conceive it and my heart can believe it, then I can achieve it."

killer TIP #28

THE CHAMPION'S MIND PART A

Killer TIP #28

In his reminiscene of the 2004 Olympic gold medal match against the CNT's Wang Hao, Ryu Seung Min of South Korea revealed his "champion's state of mind":

#1. Before the match, he admitted that he had "COMFORTABLE MIND" because he was not under too much pressure, unlike his opponent was.

#2. He never thought about defense, but always "ATTACK", always "TOP-SPIN", and always "MOVE". He said that it'd put more pressure on his opponent.

#3. He focused on "POINT BY POINT". After leading 2-1 in the match, he got full confidence.

TABLE TENNIS Killer TIPS

THE CHAMPION'S MIND PART A

#4. He always tried playing with his FOREHAND (his world famous weapon), from DEEP backhand side to DEEP forehand side.

#5. After leading 3-1 in the match and feeling confident that he'll defeat the opponent, Ryu still in fact managed to MAINTAIN HIS AGGRESSIVENESS. He was fully aware that even having a lead in a match against the CNT meant nothing and that it was still far from over!

#6. When he's leading 8-4 in the 5th game, he started THINKING of becoming an Olympic champion. Then he decided to play SAFE and to BLOCK more, which made him start to make MISTAKES. Ryu lost 11-13.

killer TIPS NETWORK

"A champion isn't made of muscle. A champion is made of heart."

killer TIP #29

THE CHAMPION'S MIND PART B

killer TIP #29

#7. Entering the 6th game with 3-2 lead, Ryu confessed that if he was forced to Game 7, he'd have "no chance". So, he tried extremely hard to CLOSE OUT the gold medal match in Game 6. And his hard work paid off!

Lesson #1. On the court, it's 100% mental, NOT techniques. The latter belongs in practice only

Lesson #2. Having a comfortable MIND takes the pressure off

A pressureless mind relaxes the body and makes it easier to FOCUS and INTENSIFY on what need to be done.

Lesson #3. When you're 100% focused, everything will "magically" CLICK together

TABLE TENNIS killer TIPS

THE CHAMPION'S MIND PART B

You'll make amazing moves and shots EASILY, EFFORTLESSLY, and INSTINCTIVELY with the RIGHT THING at the RIGHT TIME in the RIGHT WAY for the RIGHT RESULT that you won't even remember or be able to explain.

This happens ALL THE TIME in sports!

bit.ly/2luJpDk, bit.ly/2P0VII1, bit.ly/2ltVY1v, bit.ly/2ltSkF5, bit.ly/2UjKV1t, bit.ly/2UfCjUC

Lesson #4. Never let anything enter your mind. Don't throw anything into a "spinning fan"!

Lesson #5. "If you have 6 hours to chop down a tree, spend the first 4 hours to sharpen your axe." The champ did it. The "tree" is down!

killer TIPS NETWORK

> "Athletes know how to play. Champions know how to win."

killer TIP #30

THE CHAMPION'S MIND PART C

killer TIP #30

Police: "Why are you running from me?"
Driver: "Because you're chasing me!"

Ryu Seung Min: "Why are you becoming less aggressive?"
Wang Hao: "Because you're being more aggressive FIRST!"

When you're more OFFENSIVE right from the start, your opponents will likely to be more DEFENSIVE.

Regarding his Gold Medal-winning point, Ryu revealed the secret:

"In practice, I loaded up 1000's of balls each day JUST to make THAT 'gold medal' shot."

bit.ly/2Ur1mnB

TABLE TENNIS killer TIPS

THE CHAMPION'S MIND PART C

Imagine you load up 1000's of balls each day just to make your gold medal point on an ACE or a WINNER!

Imagine you load up 1000's of balls each day just to make your gold medal point on a 3RD BALL ATTACK!

The server has 100% CONTROL. A 3rd ball still gives the server 75% CONTROL.

However, once the rally is in play, the server's advantage LESSENS and EVENS OUT with the receiver's.

This is because the server's positional or strategic advantage has been NEUTRALIZED!

killer TIPS NETWORK

> "An army of sheep led by a lion would defeat an army of lions led by a sheep."

killer TIP #31
SERVING PRACTICE

killer TIP #31

If you ever think aiming at any spot along the white lines or at either corner is impossible, Jeanette *"The Black Widow"* Lee, the former number one female pool player, says that impossible is nothing when you "practice, practice, practice."

bit.ly/2IuWUBS
bit.ly/2U9QqL2

#1. With *velcro*, stick long metal rulers to cover the white lines on the three sides of the table so you can hear the result

#2. Since your first bounce determines the serve's distance, use chalk to draw two horizontal lines dividing your court into three BOUNCE ZONES.
Try to serve from each of them.

TABLE TENNIS killer TIPS

SERVING PRACTICE

#3. If you wish to have more pinpoint accuracy, experiment with this:

* Draw a circle on your court as your "BOUNCE PAD"
* Serve from the bounce pad and see where it lands on the receiver's court
* With the same chalk color, circle that "LANDING PAD"
* Try the next serve on the same bounce pad but with different direction
* Circle the new landing pad with the same chalk color, and repeat

#4. Experiment serving with different apogee and contact height between the paddle and the ball.

---

killer **TIPS NETWORK**

"Every morning in Africa, a gazelle wakes up. It knows it must run faster than the fastest lion, or it will be killed. Every morning in Africa, a lion wakes up. It knows it must run faster than the slowest gazelle, or it will starve to death. It doesn't matter whether you're a lion or gazelle, when the sun comes up, you'd better be running."

killer TIP #32
RECEIVING PRACTICE

killer TIP #32

#1. Position a ball's brand logo on its south pole. Then, with a marker, draw a circle on its north pole.

#2. Ask your practice partner to serve with the ball

#3. Once the ball is tossed, learn to focus on the BALL, not on the serve's HAND, etc.

#4. Learn to detect the spin from the TWO MARKINGS on the ball (the brand logo and your circle). The CLEARER you see the markings, the LESS SPIN and vice versa.

#5. Once your eyes can tell the ball's rotation, use an unmarked ball.

TABLE TENNIS killer TIPS

RECEIVING PRACTICE

#6. Your court's dimension is 4.5' long x 5.0' wide. When the server lands the ball close to the net, but on the thin middle line, you can attack from either the left or right side, which are both only 2.5' wide compared to the back side.

#7. In order to encourage aggression, efficiency, innovation, and perfection on both serving and receiving, practice the *"3RD BALL ATTACK CONTEST"*:

Each point must be scored either from a serve or 3rd ball attack. If the receiver manages to return the server's 3rd ball attack, the point will go to the receiver.

killer **TIPS NETWORK**

KILLERTIPS NETWORK
http://killertips.net

"I practice as if I'm playing in a game. So when the moment comes in the game, it's not new to me. You don't have to think. Instinctively, things happen!"

Michael Jordan

KILLERTIPS NETWORK
http://killertips.net

EPILOGUE

"A SPORT NOT PLAYED FOR THE GREATER GOOD

It is a fact that many countries are good at these or those Olympic sports. Some countries are even great at this or that sport.

It is also a fact that some are dominating a certain sport, such as China at table tennis, South Korea at archery, or the USA at baskeball.

It is a fact that their dominance in Olympic sports is attributed to certain factors, such as culture, ideology, historical achievements, money, etc.

It is a fact that although archery is also very popular in France, the South Korean government invests three times what their French counterparts do towards the sport.

It is a fact that at the end of the day, Olympic sports are not just sports anymore. A sport is a show business, where athletes along with the showbiz industry compete for supremacy both in the sport and in the entertainment dollar.

TABLE TENNIS killer TIPS

IS NOT WORTH PLAYING."

Sports legends and high-profile athletes are encouraged to provide "assists to achieve" for the small market sports such as table tennis.

It remains to be seen whether:

"Team Tiger Woods", *"Team Michael Schumacher"*, *"Team Eddie Jordan"*, *"Team David Beckham"*, *"Team Roger Federer"*, *"Team Cristiano Ronaldo"*, *"Team LeBron James"*, *"Team Shaquille O'Neal"*, etc.

would ever SPONSOR or ADOPT their little fellas under their wings.

These inter-sport relationships are encouraged for the love of the country, for the next generations, for the future of the sport, for becoming true role models for the world, and for all eternity.

KILLERTIPS NETWORK
http://killertips.net

www.ingramcontent.com/pod-product-compliance
Lightning Source LLC
Chambersburg PA
CBHW021954290426
44108CB00012B/1067